Still Calm

How to Manage Your Stress and Achieve Balance in Life

Dr Ann Williamson

Crown House Publishing Limited
www.crownhouse.co.uk – www.chpus.com

First published by
Crown House Publishing Ltd
Crown Buildings, Bancyfelin, Carmarthen, Wales, SA33 5ND, UK
www.crownhouse.co.uk
and
Crown House Publishing Company LLC
6 Trowbridge Drive, Suite 5, Bethel, CT 06801, USA
www.chpus.com

British Library of Cataloguing-in-Publication Data
A catalogue entry for this book is available
from the British Library.

13-digit ISBN 978-184590118-9

LCCN 2008926019

Printed and bound in the UK by

The Athenaeum Press
Gateshead

To my friend Phyllis, who travels through life gently.

Contents

Acknowledgements iii

Chapter 1   Are You A Born Worrier? 1

Chapter 2   Stress Overload? 9

Chapter 3   Half Empty Or Half Full? 17

Chapter 4   Dealing With The Stress Response 25

Chapter 5   Increasing Your Self-Confidence 47

Chapter 6   Where Do You Want To Go? 55

About the Author 69

Acknowledgements

I would like to thank all those who have contributed to my learnings over the years, and a special thanks to my husband, Iain, whose help and support made this book possible. A thank you also to my friend and colleague Dr Geoff Ibbotson, whose help and advice have proved invaluable.

Finally, last but by no means least, a very special thank you to Martin Hughes who is responsible for the cartoons in this book.

Are you a born worrier?

Chapter 1

Are You A Born Worrier?

Everyone feels anxious and stressed at some time in their lives. This book will show you ways to help yourself with these feelings and not enter the vicious cycle that may end in panic and burnout.

"I'm a born worrier," some of my patients tell me. They are wrong. You may have personality traits that make it more likely for you to become anxious, but you are not born anxious. Young toddlers do not know fear or anxiety and will run into danger until they learn. If I had no anxiety I would not bother to look both ways before crossing the road, and I would not bother to check that I've locked the front door when I go out.

So fear and anxiety have a protective value – but some people have just learnt anxiety too well.

If something has been learnt – it can be unlearnt!

We all need some anxiety to protect ourselves from danger. Anxiety only becomes a problem when, rather than feeling sensible concern, we find ourselves edging along the continuum towards panic.

Stress – Friend or Foe?

We all need some challenge in our lives or we would not be motivated to do anything. Problems arise when the demands made upon us outstrip our coping abilities. Ideally we should live our lives with a little slack in the system so that we have enough reserve to deal with emergencies or the unexpected. We may find that we are working at our peak, but then extra demands mean that we start to feel over stressed. We need to be able to detect for ourselves when this starts to happen.

Often we manage to cope during times of upheaval and crisis and then, as events settle and we expect to be able to relax and enjoy life, we begin to feel worse. Sometimes it is as though we have a delayed reaction to stressful events. This probably has survival value in that it enables us to deal with the crisis instinctively, without thinking about it. Then we allow the emotional reaction to surface when it is safe to do so.

When our stress levels are getting too high, even something very minor can tip the balance. When the jug is full, it only takes a drop or two to make it overflow. Events that we would normally take in our stride assume mountainous proportions. When our stress levels are consistently too high we tend to lose our sense of perspective and operate with much less tolerance than usual.

Our Survival Reflex

Our caveman ancestors had to contend with many dangers that threatened their very existence. Their bodies became geared up to give them what they needed for short, sharp bursts of physical activity. This meant that when threatened, they released adrenalin and other similar chemicals into their bloodstream, which helped them to fight their way out of danger or flee the scene. Adrenalin quickens the rate at which your heart beats. It makes you breathe more rapidly, thus giving you a greater supply of oxygen, and it increases your blood supply to the muscles so you can run faster. We still have this survival reflex. Adrenalin is automatically produced whenever we encounter anything our minds perceive as a threat.

Modern Stress

Unfortunately our minds perceive not only dangerous situations as threatening, but also situations in which we get frustrated and annoyed. Anxious thoughts, as well as external events, cause a release of adrenalin.

The 'What if' scenarios we often run through in our minds also generate anxiety, and therefore adrenalin. Our unconscious mind cannot distinguish between the feeling generated by an actual event and that of its anticipation.

Fight or flight are often not appropriate ways to deal with modern stress and our adrenalin levels stay high. Often the physical feelings that then ensue – such as a rapid heartbeat, palpitations, shakiness or sweating – make us feel that there is something seriously wrong with us, which leads to even more anxiety! The physical effects of adrenalin pass off within twenty minutes, but often we manage to keep producing anxiety-provoking thoughts. These keep producing more and more adrenalin, thereby prolonging the effects. No wonder people feel tired all the time when they are continually anxious! All that adrenalin makes everything work that much faster. Prolonged high levels of circulating adrenalin give rise to a whole range of physical, emotional and behavioural symptoms.

Physical Effects Of Stress

People experience the physical effects of stress in different ways. Some find it gives them feelings of nausea, and they have to keep going to the lavatory. Others feel that they can't breathe properly – they feel a tightness in their chest or a choking sensation in their throat. Still others feel shaky, or faint and sweaty. These are all effects of the adrenalin.

Other physical symptoms include headaches and migraine, sweating, palpitations, indigestion and irritable bowel syndrome. Most people, when anxious, will hold various muscles tense without being aware of it, and this can give rise to muscular aches and pains.

Eczema, psoriasis and skin irritations are commonly aggravated by stressful events. (Interestingly, both the skin and the nervous system develop from the same part of the embryo.)

Prolonged stress also reduces the efficacy of the immune system so constant minor illnesses can occur.

An almost universal symptom is feeling tired all the time. One good way of distinguishing between tiredness generated by stress and that of physical illness is how you feel when you have pushed yourself to go out – e.g. for a swim, a walk or to be with friends. If these activities make you feel a bit better, you can be fairly certain that stress is causing your tiredness. (A word of caution here: most, if not all, of these physical symptoms can have causes other than anxiety. For example, an overactive thyroid can sometimes cause sweating and shakiness. If you are at all unsure, check with your doctor. After asking you a few questions, he or she will probably be able to be fairly certain about the cause of your symptoms.)

Emotional Effects Of Stress

When people feel overstressed they often complain of poor concentration, forgetfulness, and difficulty in making decisions. You may find it hard to relax, and feel you have to be on the move all the time. Often you lose your sense of humour and feel increasing irritability and mood swings.

A stress response

Behavioural Effects Of Stress

When people have overly high levels of stress they tend to make more mistakes, are more clumsy than usual and have more accidents. You may find it more difficult to get around to doing things. You may find yourself showing more nervous habits such as nail biting and fidgeting. You may become more insistent that things should be done the way you want. Being overstressed often leads to a lack of flexibility in our approach to things.

You may notice you interrupt conversations more, or you may become more withdrawn and go out less. You may find your consumption of tobacco, alcohol and food increases – although some people lose their appetite rather than comfort-eat.

Often one of the earliest signs of becoming overstressed is an alteration in sleep patterns – having trouble falling asleep, or waking early in the morning.

Smoke Alarms

Often our nearest and dearest notice before we do that we're starting to get overstressed and irritable. It is useful to be aware of how you feel when things are beginning to get on top of you. What do **you** experience when things do not seem to be going the way you want them to? If you can listen to your own messages before events escalate, you can begin to put into practice some safety precautions that may allow you to deal with things without getting overdrawn at the stress bank!

When I start thinking longingly of solitary walks on the hills, I know it is time to look at my stressors and do something to redress the balance! Taking note of your smoke alarm can prevent the fire taking hold.

What Can I Do?

Once you have decided that your anxiety and stress levels need some attention, what can you do about it?

Basically there are three types of intervention you can use. Each will help on its own, but why not read through each of these sections and use what you feel is appropriate for you. You can't help yourself too much!

First, you can remove some of the stressors.

Second, you can alter the way you represent things to yourself – how you perceive events and how you think about things.

Third, you can learn ways of dealing with the stress response – the adrenalin you produce.

Stress review time

Chapter 2

Stress Overload?

Stress Review Time

Every now and again it is a good idea to sit down with a paper and pencil and mentally review your day. What circumstances and events triggered a feeling of anxiety or stress? Once you've written them down, look at each source of stress in your day one by one. Can you do anything about these things?

Do you see these things as challenges? If not, is it really necessary to do them? What would happen if you ditched them?

Often we cannot simply get rid of the things that stress us. If you cannot get rid of a stressor, can you perhaps alter when or how you do something so that you feel less pressured?

Sometimes it is also useful to take a broader view and look back over the last three months at the events or problems that stressed or bothered you.

Become very specific when you are analysing your stressors. Break things down into their component parts. For instance, if you feel stressed by getting the kids ready for school, break the process down into all the different tasks that make up that time in the morning: washing, getting the kids dressed, packing bags, making lunches, getting breakfast ... Is there something you could do the night before? Could you delegate something? Would getting up ten minutes earlier mean you could stay calm?

Learn to say No

If you feel stressed by caring for an elderly relative, break it down into all the elements that stress or worry you. Maybe you could find help with some things. Some things you do may not be really necessary. Some of the problems may not even be your responsibility. Often, by doing this sort of analysis, you can come up with ideas that will help to ease the situation a little.

Saying 'No'

"I cannot give you the formula for success, but I can give you the formula for failure ... which is: Try to please everybody." *(Herbert Bayard Swope)*

We all sometimes say we will do something when our intuition tells us we should really be saying 'no'.

Can we say 'no' with a smile?

Would *not* having to do something be worth the momentary discomfort of saying 'no'?

What would be the likely consequences of saying 'no'?

How would we feel if the situation were reversed and they were saying 'no' to us?

We often don't credit other people with the same amount of tolerance that we ourselves would show in the same situation.

Delegation

Can we get someone else to take on some of our load? Delegation can be difficult if you often feel you could do it quicker and better than the other person. But we learn by doing things

11

ourselves, and maybe you need to let that other person learn to do things as well as you do – even if they make mistakes at first. After all, if we didn't make mistakes, how would we improve and get better? I like this anonymous quote:

"Mistakes – a simple way to gain experience!"

Plan And Prioritise

Often when we feel pressured we tend to feel that everything has to be done at once, and it all gets too much. We then either end up doing nothing or feeling bad about all the things we haven't done yet.

Set yourself the task of doing something specific and easily achievable that needs doing each day – then, once that has been done, anything else you do that day is a bonus, and you can feel good about it!

If, after some thought, you decide a thing has to be done, then decide how urgent it is. Sit down in the evening and make a list of those things that are really urgent and need to be done the next day. Promise yourself that you will definitely do these. It is a good idea to write down three things you will definitely do the next day, and three things you might possibly do. The next day, no matter how much you don't really feel like doing them, you must make yourself do the first three – so set your goals realistically. Make your goals small to begin with.

In certain situations it helps to have three files or in-trays – one for urgent for today, one for this week and one for non-urgent – and use them accordingly!

Motivation

This may seem difficult at first, but if you make the effort it will get easier as you go on.

Imagine how things will look and feel once the task has been completed. You will motivate yourself much more easily if you focus on how good it will be when the job is done, and keep telling yourself this, or seeing the completed task in your mind's eye. Telling yourself how much you **don't** feel like doing something gives very poor motivation!

Protected Time

Make sure that you set aside uninterrupted time for important tasks. Most people find it difficult to concentrate amid continual interruptions. If you need to, take steps to ensure that you are uninterrupted – maybe put the answerphone on, perhaps tell the other people around you not to interrupt unless the building's on fire! This may seem obvious, but it's easy to expect others to mind-read and then feel annoyed when they haven't done so correctly!

Are You A Lark Or An Owl?

Some people feel much brighter and more efficient in the early morning and then flag at teatime. Others are quite the reverse, and do their best work in the evening or at night. If you think you have a definite pattern, then utilise it. Anything that requires more mental effort and concentration is better done at your peak time, whilst more routine tasks can be done when you feel less alert.

Breaks And Leisure Time

It is false economy to think you can work hard, all day, every day, without breaks. You may be able to do this for short periods, but eventually it catches up with you!

It is a very good idea to take a five- or ten-minute break in the middle of the morning and the afternoon, maybe to practise a relaxation technique (see Chapter 4), to have a short walk or simply to sit down and have a cup of tea! Never miss a lunch break; don't just snatch a sandwich while you work. Take at least half an hour, sit down to eat, preferably away from where you are working. If you feel you can't do this, then you are working too hard and probably inefficiently. Make some changes that allow you to take a lunch break.

You will work much more effectively if you make sure that you take these breaks – try it and see.

People who work at home are particularly likely to have trouble if they cannot segregate their work in some way. It may be practical to have a separate room or telephone line with an answerphone, and to keep well-defined hours during which you are available, rather than having to answer the phone twenty-four hours a day. How about turning off the mobile phone when you are not supposed to be working?

Plan for some leisure time each week. If you don't actually plan your leisure activities, then it is very easy for the time to be swallowed up by something else.

If you want to work effectively and keep your stress levels down, leisure is extremely important. Don't feel guilty about taking a little time for yourself. A relaxed and happy you is going to cope with life much better, and you will be much pleasanter to have around!

To Win Or Not To Win?

Do you always need to win? Do you always have to be the first one away when the traffic light turns green? Push yourself if it is important – if not, why not save your energy (and your petrol)!? One day when you're driving to work, instead of feeling impatient and irritated by other drivers, try feeling good when you **allow** them to overtake you or turn out in front of you. If someone does something stupid because they are going too fast, instead of swearing (which they can't hear and only raises your adrenalin levels) why not imagine that you have a spray can of pink paint and use it. As you imagine them dripping with pink paint, you may find that you are laughing inside instead of fuming! Then, taking an imaginary step backwards, wonder why they are in such a hurry. Maybe they are desperate to get to the hospital to visit an ill relative, maybe they have had some bad news and are in such a state of distress that they are not paying sufficient attention to their driving.

How do you feel about it now? Better?

(A Technique for Dealing with Road Rage by Martin Webb).

Half empty or half full?

Chapter 3

Half Empty Or Half Full?

An in-tray may be 'half full' or 'half empty'. It has the same amount of work in it, but how you represent it to yourself has an effect on how you feel about it. Words are how we represent feelings and experiences to ourselves, so the words we use internally are very important.

If you have a natural tendency to take the more pessimistic view of things, then start to be on the lookout for this and have a go at changing the words you use. Is it really 'awful' or 'terrible'? Do you really mean that? Or is it more accurately an 'annoyance' or a 'setback'? You will need to start to listen to yourself and become aware of what you are saying to yourself. This takes a little practice as our words tend to come fairly automatically, and we often hardly notice what we are saying, either out loud or internally.

Money To Burn?

Have you ever known yourself or a friend to pay good money to ride on a roller-coaster or do a bungee jump? If you have, you know how it feels – heart racing, sweating, pale, breathing fast and a knot in your stomach. Remind you of anything?

How do you feel when you get anxious and panic?

Do you remember how you felt when you fell in love for the first time and your loved one walked into the room? All these states of mind – exhilaration, infatuation, fear and anxiety – generate adrenalin release and the same kind of physical feelings in the body. **It is only the context that lends the different interpretations.**

So people pay good money to have an adrenalin burn and feel the way you do when you have a panic attack!

Panic Attacks

If you suffer from panic attacks you may find that during one you feel faint and lightheaded. Many people fear that they are going to "pass out and make a fool of myself" or even that they are dying! There are a few facts that you might find interesting to think about in this context.

The first one is that no-one ever dies from panic attacks and hardly anyone actually does faint.

The second is *why* you feel faint. When you get the adrenalin response to stress there is increased blood supply to your limbs to prepare you for fight or flight. This means that your brain may get a bit less. One of the reasons that you may feel faint is that your brain is not getting enough blood (oxygen). The body very cleverly makes you pass out so that your heart has an easier job. When you are flat on the floor your heart doesn't have to work against gravity, so blood gets up to your brain more easily!

If you were a caveman and unable to outrun or outfight the threat, then fainting would allow you to 'play dead'. This is only a secondary response after fight or flight and is definitely rather risky!

The third thing I would like you to consider is what would actually happen if you did pass out? You would fall to the floor, maybe get a bruise or two, and some onlookers might gather around. What would you think if you saw someone else faint?

Would you hurry over to see if there was anything you could do to help? Would you feel sympathetic? Or would you think, "What a fool! She must be such an idiot!"?... Point taken???

A Detective Story

If you remember, I spoke earlier about anxiety being generated by anxious thoughts as well as stressful events.

Stop a moment and become a detective for a while. **How** do you make yourself anxious? Anxious feelings don't just arise in you from nowhere, but they often happen so automatically that it seems as if they do!

Slow the process down and start to become aware of how you generate those feelings within yourself.

Are you seeing pictures of events in your mind's eye?

Maybe you are talking to yourself internally?

Maybe it is someone else's voice you hear inside?

These are the usual ways we make ourselves feel anxious.

If you become aware of the way you generate these feelings, then you can break into the pattern and interrupt it.

For instance, if you start to feel anxious the moment you wake up, you may notice that you begin your day by imagining yourself tongue-tied and embarrassed at a meeting that morning. You then start to tell yourself that it will actually happen. Once you know what's going on in your head, you can interrupt the sequence. Instead, imagine the scenario the way you would like it to run. Say something positive to yourself, or maybe jump out of bed saying, "What a wonderful day to be alive!" and remember what it feels like to be bouncy and joyful.

You may get a nauseous feeling in your stomach and a tightness in your throat, which you know means you are getting anxious. Thank your body for letting you know that you are under stress. Acknowledge the message and instead of focusing on the feelings and telling yourself that you feel really ill, tell yourself that these feelings are only caused by the adrenalin release, and will pass.

This may seem difficult at first, but, like any skill, it becomes easier with practice. Don't, however, ignore the message! Do something to help yourself feel calmer (see Chapter 4).

Never Believe Always

Start to challenge some of those almost automatic thoughts we all have. As you become aware of feeling anxious, slow yourself down and ask yourself what you are doing internally. This may seem hard at first, but it really does get easier to do as you practise!

What beliefs are you repeating to yourself? Maybe they're something like: "It's *all* going wrong! I *never* manage to do it properly!" "They *must* be whispering about me. I *know* they think I'm useless."

What evidence do you have for this? Is *everything* really going wrong? Not just the dinner or the presentation – but all your work, relationships, life, the world, your family, all your activities? Do you actually *never* manage to do it properly? *Never, ever* in any small part or degree? Whose definition of 'properly' are you looking at? Is it one that the majority of us would agree with? Has anyone complained about what you are doing? Look for evidence to support or contradict the things you are telling yourself. Could those people be whispering about a surprise birthday party? Could they actually be whispering about someone else? Have you any evidence that they think you are useless? You may be useless at something, but there are other things you do well!

Learn to challenge 'never' and 'always' when they come up in your thinking.

Must, Should And Can't!

How often do you tell yourself "I must do x", "I should do x"? Look for a moment at who says you have got to do it. What would happen if you didn't do it? Maybe try replacing 'must' and 'should' with 'like to' or 'prefer to'.

Something might always have been done in a certain way, but does that mean it has *always* got to be done the *same* way, forever?

How often do we tell ourselves, "I can't do x," and then give up without an attempt? What would happen if you could do it? Are you mind-reading again? Unless you are telepathic or can foresee the future, how can you be sure of the outcome? Would it be worth a go?

The Worry Wheel

When you feel anxious, most of your anxiety will be generated by your anticipation of events turning out badly. Thoughts take hold of us and go round and round in our minds, and nothing

The Worry Wheel

we do seems to help. It is as if we're on a hamster wheel – going nowhere.

One way of helping yourself with this is to keep a notebook and pencil in your pocket. Every time you become aware that you are on the 'wheel' with a particular worry, shout to yourself "Stop!" and clap your hands, snap a rubber band on your wrist or do anything else that comes to mind as a way of interrupting yourself. Then write the worrying thought down in your notebook. Tell yourself that you will set aside half an hour later to look at your notebook, so you don't need to think about it now. You won't forget about it because it is safely written in your notebook.

Then physically move and do something else.

Worry Time

Set aside half an hour at the end of the day to look at your notebook. As you read through the worrying thoughts that you had, ask yourself some questions.

Can I do anything about this?

If there is nothing I can usefully do, then why worry about it?

Will this still be important in a month's time? A year's time? Ten years' time?

Is this actually my problem or is it really someone else's?

These questions will help you get your worries more into perspective, and with practice you will find that you can challenge your thinking when it arises and avoid getting on the 'wheel' in the first place.

Sort Out Your Drawers!

A variation of this is to imagine a desk with three drawers in it. First of all sit down comfortably and use one of the self-hypnotic techniques described in Chapter 4. Then imagine placing the problem you are worrying about on top of the desk. As you look at the problem break it down into its parts. Any part of the problem that someone else can do something about, or that is really someone else's problem, put into the bottom drawer. Then into the middle drawer put any parts of the problem that no one can do anything about. Finally into the top drawer place the parts of the problem you can do something about. When you have cleared the top of the desk in this way, you can then open your top drawer and decide which bit to tackle first.

Chapter 4

Dealing With The Stress Response

Exercise And Time Out

One very good way of dealing with the stress response is physical exercise. This uses up adrenalin, and after exercise the body produces endorphins, which also help us to feel better, giving us a natural 'high'.

Swimming, walking, running, and going to the gym are all excellent ways of helping ourselves deal with stress.

Exercise also gives us a little 'time out' when we perhaps do not have much time to ourselves with all the different demands made on us. Time on our own, to allow us time to think, can be very useful (unless you use it to jump back on the 'worry wheel'), and so even taking a leisurely bath can be therapeutic!

Time out can also be very useful when you feel angry, as it gives you a chance to evaluate rather than leap in with an unconsidered reaction. Going for a walk rather than escalating anger upon anger in a row often leads to improved communication when the two people concerned come together again. If someone is overwhelmed with feelings of anger, they are unable to listen and evaluate what is happening. Exercise allows the body to use up the adrenalin, and then evaluation and communication stand a better chance!

Readjustment Time

It is often useful to have a break between two different stressful areas of our lives. Rather than leaving work (one potentially stressful environment) and immediately going home (another, although different, potentially stressful environment) through bad traffic (yet another stressor), consider taking a break. Maybe go for a short walk, or park up and go through a relaxation technique. Once you have had a wind-down or readjustment period you will find you cope much better!

Children often need readjustment time when returning home from school – try taking them for a short walk or a run in the park before they come home – they will behave much better for it!

Breathe!

You may notice that when you become anxious you tend to breathe with your upper chest, rather faster than normal. This is sometimes called hyperventilation and, if prolonged, may give you a tingling sensation around the lips and down the arms, and a feeling of light-headedness.

A very helpful exercise that you can practise when you are lying in bed consists of placing your hands at either side of your body just below your ribs. Focus your attention on your hands, and imagine the air flowing in and out through your hands as you breathe. You could even imagine the air has a colour if you find that helpful. After a few minutes you will notice that you are using the lower part of your chest to breathe (diaphragmatic breathing) and that you feel more relaxed.

After some practice you will find that you can do this without having your hands there, and you can do it when you are standing up or walking around.

An alternative method consists of placing your hands on your tummy and using your stomach muscles to push your hands up and down as you breathe (abdominal breathing).

Here And Now

When you are anxious you are probably either focusing on how things turned out badly in the past, or how events may shape up badly in the future. Either way, you're paying little attention to the present.

Start to focus your awareness on *now*, noticing what you are seeing, hearing, smelling and touching at this moment, and taking some pleasure in that. Take a deep, slow breath in, notice if you are holding any part of your body tense and let that tension go as you breathe out.

If you do this several times throughout the day you will start to become more aware of your muscle tension and be able to let go of it more easily. It is a good idea to use reminders to help you to remember to do this. You could tie it into each time you sit down to have a drink, or every time you open a door, or whenever you stand at the sink, go to the bathroom, etc.

Obviously, if whatever is happening now is unpleasant, it would be better not to focus your awareness on it. Use your common sense here to tell you whether this would be a useful thing to do or not. Scanning your body regularly for muscle tension is, however, quite a useful exercise to do in any case.

Stop Worrying

Have you ever wondered why just knowing that there is really no need to worry about something, and telling yourself so, never seems to help stop the worrying thoughts? We may learn to challenge our thoughts and not get stuck on the 'worry wheel', but simply telling ourselves not to worry doesn't often stop us. The model I am now going to explain may give us some answers.

A model is not the 'truth' but a possible explanation based on what we know so far, which helps us to understand what might be happening.

The brain has two halves, which tend to function fairly independently. The left half of the brain, which is responsible for our verbal and arithmetical skills, and is the source of our critical, evaluative, logical thought processes, is that part of our mind or consciousness that we are generally most aware of in our day-to-day activities.

The right side of our brain, which becomes more active as we relax, is responsible for our visual and creative imagination, the intuitive and instinctive part of ourselves. This is where we process our feelings and emotions. This part of us constantly works in the background and controls all our bodily processes such as our breathing and how fast our heart beats.

There is little communication between these two halves in our day-to-day conscious waking state.

Simply deciding at a logical (left-brain) level that you want to feel calm and then expecting to be able to achieve this as you experience a panic attack (right-brain feeling) just doesn't work. Logical reasoning doesn't get through very well, in the normal waking state, to that part of our consciousness where we process our feelings.

The brain has two halves …

But read on, and I will show you some ways that you can affect how you feel, improve your self-confidence and keep hold of that stillness within when all about you is bustle and storm.

Relaxation Techniques And Self-Hypnosis

As I mentioned earlier, in our normal waking state, our brain functions predominantly in left-brain mode. As you begin to relax, the activity begins to shift over to the right brain. The critical, evaluative thought processes (predominantly a left-brain or conscious operation) start to lessen and suggestions are more easily accepted.

This shift in brain activity occurs quite naturally throughout our day anyway. Whenever we find ourselves gazing out of the window in a daydream; driving on 'autopilot', with no conscious recollection of the last few miles; whenever we become totally focused on an activity and start to lose awareness of our surroundings, we are predominantly in a right-brain state.

I want to teach you how to access this state of mind, whenever you wish to – to bring it under your own conscious control, so that you can utilise it to help you achieve greater calmness and self-confidence.

How Can I Do That?

There are many different ways to increase your right-brain activity, and I will describe a few. Try them out and see which one feels right for you. We all experience reality differently, so what you need to do is to find your own personal 'key' to open the 'door' to your 'unconscious' right-brain.

In this way, as we start to relax or increase right-brain activity, we can start to access our unconscious mind. We can then begin to affect how we feel, and also begin to accept suggestions that will help us alter our behaviour. Remember that, as our right-brain 'thinks' in pictures, using imagery and visualisation is an effective way to access our right brain or unconscious mind. However, not everyone is good at imagining pictures in their mind's eye in glorious 3-D technicolor! This doesn't really matter, because when you think of something, or you are aware of something, you are making an image or representation at some level in your mind. How do you recognise a chair as a chair unless you compare what you see to some internal image that you have previously labelled as a chair? So, if I suggest that you visualise something, then don't feel you actually need to 'see' a picture ... just allow yourself to have an awareness.

Safety Rules – OK?

Only use these techniques when it is safe and appropriate to do so – never in the driving seat of a car. You don't want to link a relaxed hypnotic state with sitting in the driver's seat. Always stop the car, pull over and move over to the passenger seat.

If an emergency occurs whilst you are relaxing, you can get up immediately and deal with it, but, as you focus internally, your awareness of what is going on outside of you will decrease. In the same way as you can shut sounds out when you get absorbed in a good book, you may still hear sounds around you, but they become less intrusive.

Become used to getting into a relaxed state both while sitting and while lying down. If you always practise sitting in an armchair, you will find it harder to do it lying on your bed. The brain loves to make links.

Whenever you use a formal self-hypnotic or relaxation technique, there are a few precautions that it is wise to take. Always tell yourself before you start how long you want to relax for, because when you become practised at doing these types of exercises you may get quite deeply relaxed and experience time distortion. You may feel you have only been relaxing for ten minutes when half an hour has actually passed. This could be very inconvenient, so tell your unconscious mind how long you want to relax for and trust it to give you notice when that time has elapsed. If you are using these techniques to help you fall asleep, then tell yourself you are going to relax for a few minutes and then drift off into a natural sleep, from which you will awake feeling refreshed and relaxed. If you are overtired, any relaxation technique may send you to sleep. If this is not desirable, make sure you set an alarm before you start.

What Is It Like?

Everyone is different, so each person will experience a trance-like state differently. You may feel relaxed, and that can be very enjoyable, but you don't **have** to feel relaxed. An athlete focusing internally before and during a race is far from relaxed, but is still in that trance-like right-brain state.

Some people experience a feeling of heaviness, some a feeling of lightness, some may feel warm and tingly, others may lose awareness of where their arms and legs are resting. Whatever you feel is fine, and right for you.

Some people find getting into 'right-brain activity' easier than others, but, as with any skill, it can improve with practice. If this is unfamiliar to you, I would recommend you practise for five or ten minutes, maybe twice a day, for the first three to four weeks.

The time spent in this way is more than made up by your improved effectiveness and concentration as you feel less stressed or anxious. You can start to become the master, rather than the victim, of your emotions.

A Self-Hypnotic Technique

One popular way of achieving this relaxed, trancelike state is through progressive muscular relaxation. Read through the description below, and then see whether this particular method suits you. You might find it easier to read it into a cassette recorder and then listen to it whilst following the instructions.

A Progressive Muscular Relaxation Technique

Perhaps you would like to make yourself comfortable. Place your feet firmly on the floor, and let your hands just rest easily on your lap. If you prefer, you could lie down somewhere comfortable.

I would like you now to take a deep breath in, and as you breathe out just let your body go loose and slack, like a rag doll.

Just let all the tensions drain away with each outgoing breath.

As you breathe out, you can let your eyes close and focus on the muscles of your head and face and neck.

Let the muscles of your head and face and neck go loose and slack. Become aware of your forehead, very wide and smooth. Become aware of the space within your mouth, of the position of your tongue. Notice the muscles of your throat relax as you swallow. You might like to imagine a colour or a warm glow drifting down your body from the top of your head as you begin to relax.

Let a feeling of comfort drift gently down into your neck and shoulders. Let the muscles around your shoulders go loose and slack, let the relaxation drift down your arms right to your fingertips.

Let your arms feel heavy and comfortable. You might notice a tingling feeling or a feeling of warmth in your hands as they relax.

Let the muscles around your chest relax, let the feeling of comfort spread down into the muscles of your back and stomach. Let the muscles of your tummy go loose and slack as that colour drifts down.

Let any outside noises just recede into the background and contribute to a feeling of safety and comfort.

Enjoy just being, instead of having to be doing.

Let the muscles of your legs go loose and slack, let them feel really heavy, sinking down like two lead weights to the floor as the relaxation spreads down, right down to your toes. Let the tensions drain out of the soles of your feet into the floor.

Become aware of your breathing; maybe imagine breathing in a colour and notice it spreading throughout your body as you relax, letting go of any tension as you breathe out. Just enjoy that lovely comfortable feeling, letting go with each

A self-hypnosis technique

outgoing breath to become just as deeply relaxed as you want to be.

A Special Place

I would like you now to imagine a very special place, a place where you can feel completely relaxed and safe and calm.

Let your conscious mind wonder what place your unconscious mind will find for you.

It may be a place you have visited, or it may be a place that your mind finds for you. It may be inside or outside.

Look all around you, notice the colours, whatever you can see.

Smell any smells that might be there.

Hear any sounds that might be in the place you have chosen, and look to see where they are coming from.

Begin to notice the texture of what you are standing or resting on, the temperature of the air around you. Above all, feel the peace and calmness of the place you have chosen.

Really experience this special place, because this is your own special place that no one can take from you, a place where you can go to when you need to relax, to recharge your batteries, a place where any suggestions you give yourself will sink straight into your unconscious mind and begin to exert an effect on how you think and how you feel and how you behave.

Each time you use these techniques it will become easier to become even more relaxed, even more quickly.

Coming Back To The Here And Now

Enjoy those feelings of relaxation and calmness and, in a few minutes, when you are ready, you can gradually come back to the here and now.

You can count yourself back in your head from five to one, taking the time you need, so that by the time you reach one you are wide awake, feeling refreshed and alert with all your sensations back to normal, but keeping hold of that feeling of calmness within.

Other Ways You Could Use

There are many, many alternative methods

■ One way you might like to try for yourself consists of closing your eyes and holding one arm out in front of you, focusing your attention on your arm and hand. Imagine that they are feeling heavier and heavier as you become more and more deeply relaxed. Just allow your arm to gradually come down to your lap, without any conscious effort on your part. By the time your arm reaches your lap you are feeling really comfortable and relaxed and ready to go to your special place (see page 36). As your arm touches your lap you can allow its weight to come back to normal.

■ You could rest one hand with your fingertips just lightly touching your knees and imagine a large helium-filled balloon (what colour is it?) tied to your wrist. As you imagine that arm and hand getting lighter and lighter and the pull of the balloon getting stronger and stronger, you can begin to feel more and more relaxed. You may find your hand starting to float up off your knees as you become really focused on the pull of the balloon as it tugs at your arm ... floating up and up like a feather ... without you having consciously to do anything at all.

... After a while you can imagine untying the balloon and watching it float away into the distance as you become more and more relaxed ... maybe carrying away something you would like to get rid of ...

... You can, if you like, allow your hand to float up and up, your arm bending at the elbow, until your fingers touch your face. Then, as your arm gradually regains its normal weight and comes back down to your lap, you can really enjoy that feeling of relaxation getting deeper and deeper until you are ready to go to your special place (see page 36).

■ Another method you could try is to hold your hands out in front of you, with their palms facing and about nine inches apart, and imagine that you have a magnet in each palm. Imagine feeling the pull between the two magnets. As your hands move closer and closer together, the pull becomes stronger and stronger and you become more and more deeply relaxed, until, as they touch, you are ready to go to your special place (see page 36). Then, as your hands gradually come down to your lap, you can allow yourself to feel more and more comfortable and relaxed.

■ Maybe you could just take five deep breaths, counting each one in turn, allowing yourself to relax with each outgoing breath. Maybe imagine breathing in a colour, and imagine it spreading throughout your body as it relaxes until you are ready to go to your special place (see page 36).

■ You could simply close your eyes and take yourself back to some place or some activity that you enjoy, and relive the experience – feeling, seeing, smelling and hearing what is happening. For example, lying in the warm sunshine, looking up at the clouds, with the smell of fresh-cut grass and the scents of wild flowers around you. Maybe imagining your favourite piece of music playing, as you feel more and more relaxed. You could then go to your special place if you wished to do so (see page 36).

■ You could actually listen to some music that you feel is appropriate, closing your eyes and enjoying the internal images and feelings that it generates within you until you feel you are ready to go to your special place (see page 36).

Use your imagination to find the best way for you to focus internally, and tie that into becoming more and more relaxed. You could use one of the methods described above or string several together to become as deeply relaxed as you are comfortable with.

If you have felt very tense for a long time, you have probably forgotten just how your muscles can feel when they are relaxed. In this situation you might prefer to close your eyes and take yourself back in your imagination to an activity that you enjoyed, such as swimming or riding. Re-experience that fully: seeing, hearing, smelling, feeling just how it was. As you do this, you will find that your body will begin to relax as your mind becomes totally absorbed in enjoying the experience you have chosen.

Troubleshooting

The main problem people have with these kind of techniques is that they 'try' too hard. Why not allow your conscious mind to 'wonder' what will happen, and then just see what happens?

Don't worry if stray thoughts cross your mind whilst you are doing these exercises. Allow the thought to float in, and then out, but instead of following it, bring yourself back to what you were doing. Alternatively, start counting backwards from three hundred in sevens until you feel ready to continue!

Occasionally, if you have been suppressing various sad emotions, you might start to feel upset and shed a tear as you relax. This doesn't happen often, but you can tell yourself that by expressing that feeling you have dealt with whatever it was that caused it. It is a good idea then to relax again and purposefully think of a happy memory and take yourself back there, getting fully in touch with good feelings before returning to the here and now. If you feel that you have a problem that you need some help with, please go and see a properly qualified therapist or your own doctor.

Remember that practising this skill will enable you to get better and better at it. When you are used to accessing this relaxed state, you will probably find that you don't really need to go through a long routine, but you can slip easily and effortlessly into it with a few breaths.

Why Bother?

Just sitting down and spending ten minutes a day using a self-hypnotic relaxation technique will help reduce your anxiety levels and bring your adrenalin levels back to normal. But why not utilise the increased access to your unconscious that you have in this state to help you to stay calm and to achieve greater feelings of self-confidence and well-being? Just going into trance and not using it to give yourself positive suggestions is a bit like having an anaesthetic without the surgery – rather a waste of time! So read on ...

Discarding Negative Feelings

By using imagery (or pictures) you can help yourself to off-load anxieties and negative feelings and get in touch with good, positive feelings to replace them. Using imagery whilst you are in a relaxed state enables your suggestions to affect your unconscious mind and thereby to have an effect on how you feel and behave. (Remember, your unconscious or right brain 'thinks' in pictures and symbols.)

You could imagine walking down some steps as you become more deeply relaxed, down to a bridge over a river. You could stop halfway over the bridge, to throw away any unwanted negative thoughts or feelings into the river and watch them being washed away. Or you could imagine throwing those negative thoughts down a rubbish chute, flinging them onto a bonfire, or tying them to a balloon and watching them drift away ... Allow your imagination to find the right image for you.

Discarding negative feelings

Back To The Drawers

You may remember that in Chapter 3, I suggested that one way you could imagine organising and breaking down your worries was by using a desk with three drawers. A useful way of using imagery in trance would be to imagine your desk and start to tidy it up. The desk could represent your life and have many different drawers. Allow your unconscious mind to show you what is appropriate for you. There could be a handy waste-paper basket for you to throw unwanted rubbish into. Maybe you want to tidy the top of your desk, or perhaps one or more of the drawers. Let your unconscious mind be your guide here.

Giving Positive Suggestion – Verbally

Please, can you **not** think of a red bicycle? Of course you can't. In order not to think 'red bicycle' you have to think of it first. It becomes easier if I ask you instead of a 'red bicycle' to think of a 'yellow car'!

In order not to feel anxious, you want to feel calm, so instead of suggestions such as "I don't want to feel panicky" it is better to tell yourself that you would like to feel "calm and in control". Suggestions should preferably be stated in the positive – what you want, rather than what you don't want.

You could just give yourself verbal suggestions whilst you are in your special place such as ...

Each day I will become more relaxed and calm, more confident and in control. I will become so deeply interested in whatever I am doing or whoever I am with that my problems will bother me less and less. This feeling of calmness and peace, this feeling of confidence, will mean that I have more energy to do all the things that I want to do. I will see things more clearly, without distortion, more in perspective, and each day this feeling of confidence and calmness will grow, so that as each day passes I will feel and act with more confidence, I will feel more calm and relaxed ... I will feel fitter and healthier ... and be able to use my inner resources to help me to do and be whatever is right for me as a whole person.

Giving Positive Suggestions – Using Imagery

Decide before you go into trance what positive suggestions you want at this particular time. Generally, feelings of calmness, confidence, optimism and energy are the kinds of things you might wish to focus on.

Find some way of seeing your positive suggestions in your special place, maybe on a notice-board, written on rocks or drawn on the ground. You could use the imagery of a small, still pool, very peaceful and calm, to represent your 'pool of internal resources'.

As you sit and gaze at the water, enjoying the sound of silence, or whatever sounds you experience, you notice that on the bottom of the pool are various stones and pebbles. These represent all the strengths and resources you already have, and you can feel pleased and encouraged as your unconscious mind identifies each resource, even though your conscious mind may not know what they are. Some you may have forgotten about, and others you may not even know you have yet, and you can begin to feel excited at all the things you will achieve with all these resources.

Around the edge of your pool are various stones that represent other positive feelings or resources, or those that you may want even more of. Decide what you want – maybe physical relaxation, mental calmness or peace of mind, or feelings of confidence in yourself and your ability to be whatever you want to be. Pick up a stone that represents what you want (your unconscious mind will let you know which stone is the right one). Study the stone carefully, noticing its shape, texture, colour and weight. Then drop it into your pool, watching it drift gently down through the clear water to settle safely and securely on the bottom.

Using these kinds of positive suggestion regularly whilst doing your self-hypnosis will gradually (sometimes very quickly!) build up your ability to remain calm and cope with increasing stress without anxiety.

Increasing self-confidence

Chapter 5

Increasing Your Self-Confidence

The way you feel depends on the pictures you make in your mind's eye and the words you hear internally.

If you *see* yourself as worried, harassed and failing miserably to cope with your day-to-day life, *and you keep telling* yourself that inside, then this will indeed be the way you will tend to behave.

If, on the other hand, you *see* yourself as coping calmly and confidently and *tell yourself* that you are feeling like that, then that is how you will begin to behave.

You cannot hold two opposing images and feelings in your mind at one time.

Improving Your Self-Image

Regularly practise seeing yourself the way you want to be. Close your eyes and settle down in whatever way you have found best for yourself, and imagine seeing an image of yourself the way you don't want to be behind you. Make it a dull, unattractive image. Then, in front of you imagine the you the way you do want to be. Step into that you, feel how good it feels, say to yourself that you are pleased to be moving in the right direction, and open your eyes. Repeat this several times until the image behind you fades or becomes less distinct.

Making Links

If you think of cutting a lemon in half and squeezing out the juice – what happens? You salivate. A visual image has caused a physical effect. This reaction is based on your previous experience and memories of lemons. If you had no prior knowledge of a lemon you would not begin to salivate.

We all know that smells, sounds, or seeing something can trigger memories. When we remember an event we also re-experience some of the feelings associated with it. Wouldn't it be good if we could instantly bring to mind a good feeling whenever we needed it? You can learn to do precisely that!

Try standing up to attention, with your shoulders back, and raise your level of sight so that you are looking up – and feel the effect of a positive link you have already built up over so many years that it is now a part of your physiology. Try to feel harassed and anxious whilst in this position, and you will find it much harder to do!

Make the muscle movements of a smile when you feel down, and after a few moments notice the effect on how you feel as that feeling in your facial muscles links you back to happier feelings.

If you use a special place to go to in your mind when you relax, then after a while, just thinking of this visual image will get you in touch with some of those feelings of calmness that have become linked in your mind to that place.

Building A Confidence Trigger

You can build a confidence trigger for yourself by closing your eyes, relaxing and allowing your unconscious mind to come up with the memory of a time when you felt things went just the way you wished.

A time when you felt confident and in control, when you felt good inside and out.

As you re-experience that event and feel those feelings, anchor them. Do this by pressing a finger and thumb together, making a fist with your dominant hand, and/or allowing a visual symbol or internal sound to come into your mind as you feel the feeling. This will create a link to those feelings and/or that memory. It is important that you imagine yourself back in the memory, really reliving it, not merely seeing it as a picture of an event with you in it. Allow the good feeling to build and make your fist, etc. as the feeling reaches its height. Do not anchor the feelings when they are fading away.

Finding A Memory

Some people find it difficult to remember a time when they felt confident, but everyone has some positive event they can go back to. Maybe it's the first time you swam a width at the swimming pool or completed the obstacle race at school, or maybe the very first time you baked a cake and it rose in the middle instead of sinking!

If you really have difficulty, then use your imagination. What might it be like to climb a very steep hill and finally reach the top, where you can see the view spread out before you and feel the wind in your hair. You could imagine what it might feel like to win a race and have everyone cheering you on ...

Remember that it is the feeling of being in control and of feeling confident that you want to tie into a trigger, so anything you can do internally to increase the feelings will help. Make the colours bright, bring out the sun, make it even better than you actually remember. Maybe surround the swimming pool with cheering onlookers as you swim your width! Use your imagination and above all, ENJOY IT!

Build It Up

Repeat this with the same memory, or some other appropriate memories, and maybe build on your trigger each time you do your self-hypnosis. Whenever you wish, allow yourself to settle into trance and then go back to the same memory or a different memory of a suitable time and link the feelings to your trigger by clenching your fist, etc. Remember, just as a muscle becomes more powerful with use, your trigger will be more effective if it's used often. The more often your mind makes that link between those good feelings and your trigger, the more automatic it will become.

Doing this will mean that you have those feelings of confidence at your fingertips, to use whenever you feel you have the need. If you have a visual image that links you to good feelings, then keep looking up and imagining it. The more often you do this, the easier it will be when you are feeling anxious.

You might like to build yourself a couple of anchors or triggers. Maybe one for calmness, and one for confidence or assertiveness?

Whenever something happens where you feel particularly calm or confident, then hook that good feeling onto your anchor as well!

Time For Fun?

How about a humour anchor? Laughter always makes you feel better, and being able to inject a little fun or humour into a situation usually helps. Can you feel worried and panicky, and feel like laughing at the same time? I don't mean 'hollow laughter' but the feeling you get inside when you find something really funny. As well as being a happy feeling, it is one that is very good for you! An old Chinese proverb says "He who laughs lasts!"

Whistle A Happy Tune!

Can you recall a time when you were little and feeling a bit scared – did you sing or whistle to help yourself feel better? Singing occupies both right (melody) and left (words) sides of the brain, so there is less room for fear. A very useful tip if you are feeling anxious and panicky is to sing a well-known nursery rhyme or song in your head, over and over. "Baa, Baa Black Sheep" is a good one to use!

Panic Attack Controls

It is all very well being able to sit down for ten minutes and gradually feel better as you do your self-hypnosis, but what can you do when you need instant help?

You can use your anchors, of course. You could also practise diaphragmatic breathing, or taking deep, slow breaths and letting the tension go with each outgoing breath. Other methods you could use are imagining the word 'CALM' written in the air above you. Then as you say the word 'Calm, calm, calm' to yourself, imagine it dripping down (maybe like drips of paint) onto your head, and as it flows down your body imagine it pushing

Sing away the panic!

the panic before it, down your body and out of your feet. Some people like to imagine a colour they associate with calmness gradually flowing through their body.

Secret Calm

If you are very busy at work and beginning to feel harassed, this is an exercise you can do very simply, every hour on the hour. Look at a spot, maybe on your desk, and take a deep breath in. As you breathe out, imagine yourself feeling floppy, like a rag doll, and imagine being in your 'special place' (see page 36). Gather up some good feelings and bring yourself back to the here and now with them. There is no need to close your eyes, and the whole thing may only take a minute, but it gives you a 'time out' to allow yourself to relax and refocus.

Chapter 6

Where Do You Want To Go?

A Slug Story

There were once two slugs who one day found themselves sitting on a metal lid in the sunshine. One slug said to the other, "I am getting very hot. I wish a cloud would come and cover up the sun." He crawled around and around in aimless circles and fried.

The other slug thought, "He's right. It is getting hot. I'd better move off, or I'll fry!" And so he turned and crawled off. It didn't much matter which direction he took – any way got him off the metal plate!

Everest – Step By Step

When you start to think about what you want to do, you need to be quite specific. It's not much use just thinking, "I want to be better." What would you be doing differently? What are you not doing now, that you want to do? It is important also to break large goals down into smaller components. Everest is climbed by putting one foot in front of the other – but you do need a map!

Setting A Goal

Did you know that the bumblebee cannot fly? Aerodynamically and scientifically, it is impossible for the bumblebee to fly – but nobody told it so! Hence it can, and does, fly with ease!

At one time it was thought that it was humanly impossible to run a four-minute mile. Roger Bannister proved it possible, and very shortly afterwards several others reached and surpassed the supposedly 'impossible'.

We tend to only use a small percentage of our inner resources and abilities at any one time, and often our 'conscious' doubts keep us from achieving all that we could possibly do. We tell ourselves, "Oh, I can't do that," so we fail.

If we set ourselves a goal whilst in a relaxed state (in touch with our unconscious mind), we start to mobilise all the unconscious resources we need to achieve that goal. By visualising how we want to be, we are helping our brain to write the 'programme' that will help us to achieve it.

You get what you expect to get … so decide what you want, and then … GO FOR IT!

How To Set Your Goal

1. Relax in whatever way you feel best for you, and maybe go to your 'special place' (see page 36).

    Make an image of yourself the way you want to be, doing whatever you decide to do. Make it a 'feeling' picture, and have some way of seeing the target date, e.g., a newspaper or a calendar on the wall. Maybe see yourself telling a friend that you have achieved your goal.

    When the image is clear, go 'into' the image, making any adjustments that you feel are desirable. Notice what you smell, hear and see, and feel how good it feels to have achieved your goal.

Gradually bring yourself back to the here and now, knowing that your unconscious mind will mobilise the resources you need to achieve your goal.

Remember that, so far as your unconscious mind is concerned, you now not only have the T-shirt, but have already worn it!

Or:

2. Close your eyes, relax and imagine that you are sitting on a road in the present. Imagine the past running off into the distance – last week, last month, last year and all the way back to your beginning, in one direction. Imagine the future – tomorrow, next month, next year, running off into the distance in the other direction.

   Make an image (a feeling picture) of you having achieved your goal. Step into the image and adjust how it looks (maybe brighten the colours, or add movement) until it feels just right. Make it as good as it can possibly be! Step out of the picture.

   Take the image and float above 'now'. Energise the picture with four deep breaths, and imagine floating up and above your road into the future and dropping the image into the appropriate place on your 'time' road.

   Float back to 'now' and come back to the here and now with the certainty that your unconscious mind will mobilise the resources you need to achieve your goal.

   If you cannot see your goal, or if it feels uncomfortable, then you need to look again at your decision to have that as your goal. Maybe you need to readjust it.

As you progress towards your goal you will consciously become aware of the steps that you need to take to achieve it, because your unconscious mind has now assessed the situation and knows which way you want to go.

Positive Mental Rehearsal

I have already talked about the 'What if?' scenarios that we use in our minds to make ourselves feel anxious. Stop and think about it for a moment – if you are feeling very anxious, you are functioning in a more right-brained state than usual. By making pictures in your mind of the unpleasant possibilities and focusing on these, you are, in effect, giving yourself powerful negative suggestions. Once you have looked at what you can do to prevent the catastrophes from occurring and have taken any sensible steps that are necessary, why not have a go at doing the opposite?

When you have worrying thoughts about an event, e.g. an examination, try using your self-hypnosis. Settle down and imagine the outcome that you want, e.g. walking out after the examination feeling satisfied that you have done your best. When you have a clear image or awareness of this, imagine seeing, hearing and feeling what would be appropriate in that situation. Maybe imagine telling a friend how well the exam has gone. By focusing on the outcome you want rather than anticipating and focusing on what you don't want to happen, you are much more likely to achieve your goal.

As well as making images of how you want to be, in trance, you can also make images of yourself in different situations, behaving and feeling the way you want to.

1. Close your eyes and relax.

2. Imagine yourself feeling calm and relaxed, e.g. whilst being at the dentist.

3. Step into the image and feel good about how you are feeling, and say something appropriate to yourself in your head, e.g. "I am pleased that I feel calm and in control."

4. Open your eyes.

5. Close your eyes and repeat steps 2, 3, and 4 several times.

It is a good idea to practise this daily when you do your self-hypnosis.

Problem People

Here's a thought ...

If you always do what you've always done, you'll always get what you've always got.

If we always react towards someone in a particular way, we will tend to provoke the same response. When we talk to someone, only about 7 per cent of our communication is the words we utter. Around 13 per cent of our communication lies in the tone of our voice. A massive 80 per cent of our communication lies in our body language, most of which we are not aware of consciously. When we communicate with someone, they react to the totality of our communication. If we change our body language then their response to us will inevitably change in some way.

We can use this to help us improve how we communicate with someone we have difficulty with. Our body language is affected by how we feel about the person we are communicating with. We have in our minds a representation or coded memory of that person. If we change how we code or represent that person, we will change how we feel and react towards them.

First of all imagine the person you maybe find threatening or irritating and ask yourself the following questions.

How far away from me is the image?

Is it in colour or black and white?

Is the image bright or dim?

Is it clearly focused or blurred?

Is it still or moving?

Is it life-sized? Smaller? Larger?

Is the image on its own or does it have a background?

Then imagine someone you don't have any strong feelings about, but that you get on with reasonably well, and repeat the questions. You will almost certainly find that the way you represent these two people to yourself is different in several respects.

The next stage of the process is to return to the image of the person you have a problem with and change the relevant factors to match the second image.

For instance, the first image may be very close, brightly coloured, clearly in focus, moving, larger than life.

The second image may be farther away, less bright but still coloured, slightly blurred, still and life-sized.

Try changing each factor in turn and notice how it affects the 'feel' of the image.

First, move the image farther away. If that makes it feel less threatening, that's fine — keep the change. If it makes no difference, put it back to how it was before.

Tone down the brightness and notice whether that has an effect.

Make the image slightly blurred. Any effect?

Stop the image moving and notice whether, when the image is still, it feels more comfortable.

Shrink the image to life-sized and again notice the effect on your feelings.

You may have noticed other differences, such as whether the images are full-face or profile, whole body or head and shoulders. See if changing these has any effect and each time keep the change if it makes the image feel more comfortable. If it doesn't, put it back.

Then practise imagining the 'problem' person with the changes that you have determined makes your representation of that person feel more comfortable. This will affect your unconscious body language when you next encounter that person, and so alter your communication. You may not like them any better, but you may find dealing with them somewhat easier.

If you find someone's voice a problem, you can do something very similar with how you represent such factors as pitch, rhythm, pace, loudness, etc.

Defusing Anger

Anger, whether justified or not, can be a very destructive emotion. Feelings of anger make it much more difficult to deal effectively with someone. It is also much harder to be assertive if you feel uncontrolled anger.

There are various ways you can help yourself in this situation. You could for example, ventilate your feelings in some way. This might be by writing or drawing whatever comes into your mind as you feel the anger. You would not necessarily show this to anyone – just putting your feelings down on paper can help you to let them go.

Some people have found it useful to buy some bread-mix (or make their own!), project their anger into the dough and enjoy pummelling it. This method also gives you a good loaf of bread as a by-product!

You could also use trance to help you get rid of anger through using imagery. Imagine that you are driving miles and miles away from anywhere to some rocky place. Once there, imagine finding a large boulder and project your anger onto it, maybe mark it in some way. Then look around and find some way of smashing it up. This could be with a pneumatic drill, a sledgehammer or even some dynamite! Enjoy the process of smashing it up. Shout or swear at it if you want (in your imagination, not out loud)! Once it is in tiny pieces decide what to do with them – maybe sweep them up and throw them away? Then, and this is most important, go to some calm relaxing place in your imagination and gradually let the peace of the place you have chosen fill you entirely. Then, when you are ready, bring yourself back to the here and now.

Defusing anger

Assertiveness

The golden rule here is to express your feelings calmly before they run away with you! Express how you feel by saying "I am starting to feel upset" rather than "You are making me upset." It is important simply to state how you are feeling without apportioning blame. Then state what you would like the other person to do and how you might feel when that has happened.

Taking a moment or two to put yourself in the other person's position and feel how they might be feeling can also be useful. Taking a look at a situation from a distance often means that you can see things that may not be immediately obvious when you are in the thick of it.

Criticism And Praise

Most of us are our own worst enemy when it comes to putting ourselves down. Self-criticism may be useful if it is realistic and constructive, but too often we are overly critical and neglect to redress the balance with some self-congratulation!

Good managers know that, to get the best out of someone, any criticism needs to be sandwiched between praise or some other positive statement.

We know that children respond more readily to reward than punishment. So how often do we praise or reward ourselves when we do something right? Not often, at a guess!

If we have a negative parrot on one shoulder telling us that whatever we do is rubbish, then let us at least have a positive parrot on the other shoulder to redress the balance! Why not start to make a point of congratulating yourself internally when appropriate?

If you have just completed some task that you really didn't want to do, then how about giving yourself a reward?

A Final Story

You are walking along a beautiful beach. The waves are breaking gently on the edge of the sands. You can hear the seagulls calling and smell the salt sea. The sun is shining, and there is just a little breeze, making the temperature just right for you. As you walk along, feeling the warm sand between your toes, you notice that every now and then there are some pebbles lying on the sand. Mostly they look grey and uninteresting, but you notice one over there that is different and seems special to you in some way. You pick it up and put it in your pocket to take with you.

As you continue, you look at the seashells and notice that most of them have been broken into small pieces by the wind and the waves. But every so often you come across a whole one, maybe a gently spiralling whelk shell, or an oyster shell flushed with pink. Maybe you would like to put them in your pocket also.

Farther along the beach, in the rockpools, you look at the seaweed. Most of it is that rather uninteresting brown rubbery sort, but now and again you notice a beautiful green frond waving in the water. You could take a piece of this with you, if you wish.

As you walk farther, enjoying the smell and the sounds of the sea, a piece of driftwood catches your eye. It's a strangely twisted shape, bleached white by the sun and worn smooth by the waves. You decide to take it back with you.

You complete your walk and take your treasures home with you. Time passes, and you forget all about your treasure hunt along the seashore.

The scene changes to a garden. In your garden there is a trellis, and at its base is planted the seed of a vine. The rain falls and the sun shines and slowly the seed germinates. It pushes its roots down into the soil, gathering water and nourishment, and slowly raises its head up above the earth. First one leaf unfurls and then another. Growing bigger every day to catch the sunlight, it starts to send out tendrils that catch onto the trellis. They cling to the trellis and it lends the vine support as it grows.

Days pass, and weeks pass, and the vine grows and spreads across the trellis, its branching stems bearing beautiful green leaves.

Suddenly the vine comes to a break in the trellis. The tendrils wave about, trying to find somewhere to go or something to support them. Luckily, the gardener is a careful gardener and notices the gap in the trellis.

You remember the old piece of driftwood you picked up all that while ago on the beach and you realise that it is perfect for the job. You tie it in place, and it bridges the gap beautifully.

The vine continues to grow in strength and vigour. It spreads across the gap that used to be in the trellis and begins to flower.

As the vine grows stronger and sturdier one might begin to wonder if the trellis is supporting the vine or the vine the trellis – but it doesn't really matter.

The vine becomes home to many small animals, and birds find nesting places within its branches. Eventually the vine starts to bear fruit and its branches become heavy with bunches of grapes. It continues to mature and grow and be fruitful over many, many years, and the gardener is content.

Finale

You may like to do this exercise in your head, but I find it is often more powerful to actually walk it out on the floor, so I will describe it as if this is the way you are doing it. It is also a very useful way to help you to get out of a negative state if you feel 'stuck'.

First, stand up. This is position 1 – you, the way you are now.

Now, in front of where you are standing, imagine yourself the way you would like to be. This is position 2. Make it a really good feeling image.

Then step to one side – position 3, where you can 'see' both images 1 and 2. From this position you are in touch with all the resources you need. You can 'go inside' and see exactly what resources you need to move from 1 to 2. Allow your unconscious mind to gather those resources and project them to you at position 1.

Then move back to position 1 and accept the resources from your 'higher self' and integrate them fully into yourself.

Then you can move triumphantly into position 2 feeling the way you want to feel, behaving the way you want to behave, and above all, feeling how good it is to be the way you want to be. Allow yourself to really experience this, and then reorientate yourself back to the here and now, bringing with you all the good feelings you have just experienced.

Remember ...

You have all the resources within you to become the person you wish to be!

About The Author

Dr Ann Williamson has been a General Practitioner for thirty two years and has used hypnosis for more then fifteen years to help her patients deal with stress and anxiety and to help them facilitate change in how they live their lives.

She is an Accredited member of the British Society of Medical & Dental Hypnosis (now BSCAH, the British Society of Clinical & Academic Hypnosis), a certified NLP Master Practitioner and has had training in brief solution oriented therapy and other approaches. She has been involved for many years with teaching Health Professionals how to use hypnotic techniques both for themselves and within their own field of clinical expertise. She runs workshops on stress management, personal development and brief psychological interventions on request, as well as seeing private clients for therapy. She also lectures at Manchester, Chester and Salford Universities and runs Creative Wellbeing weekends which combine stress management and the expressive arts.

For more details on workshops and on hypnosis and self hypnosis please visit www.annwilliamson.co.uk
or contact the British Society of Clinical & Academic Hypnosis (BSCAH) on 0844 8843116 or www.bscah.co.uk